# GOD DELIVERS
## *More Than*
## *Just*
# PACKAGES!

MICHELLE KNUDSON

WESTBOW
PRESS®
A DIVISION OF THOMAS NELSON
& ZONDERVAN

WestBow Press books may be ordered through booksellers or by contacting:

WestBow Press
A Division of Thomas Nelson & Zondervan
1663 Liberty Drive
Bloomington, IN 47403
www.westbowpress.com
844-714-3454

ISBN: 978-1-6642-1442-2 (sc)
ISBN: 978-1-6642-1441-5 (e)

Library of Congress Control Number: 2020923869

Print information available on the last page.

WestBow Press rev. date: 12/11/2020

# CONTENTS

# DEDICATION

I would like to dedicate this book first of all to the Lord, who despite my incessant whinging and tantrums, never gives up on me and has taught me how to love without reservation. Lord, thank you for everything good in my life. May this book give you glory!

To my husband Gary, whose unconditional love and support has brought so much joy and happiness into my life, and to our three boys who always encouraged me to rely on God when I was given a hard route.

Lastly, to my mother Victoria, who played a huge role in helping me find the path God wanted me to take and who continually encourages me to never give up.

# INTRODUCTION

Our family was on vacation in Chelan, Washington, a place we typically go when we need to get away and rest. I was sitting in the back bedroom of our condo, watching videos on YouTube about a program where I could learn to deliver packages directly to people's doors. As I watched those videos, I thought, *I can do this!* I shared my thoughts with my husband, explaining how I thought this could benefit us. He was a little hesitant, not fully understanding how this program worked and how I was supposedly going to learn it. Little did we both know that God had a plan to change my life completely with this program, not to mention take His relationship with me to a whole new level of faith and trust. God delivered all these things with Amazon.

# WHAT IS AMAZON?

Amazon is a global company, founded by Jeff Bezos in 1994, that specializes in online retail shopping services. The firm's North American segment provides both online retail services and subscriptions through their main websites, www.amazon.com and www.amazon. ca. Amazon's international web services include global sales of computers, databases, and storage for government agencies, business start-ups, academic institutions, and enterprises.[1]

---

[1] Forbes, accessed October 23, 2020, https://www.forbes.com/companies/ amazon/#73fdc6866fb8.

Amazon is listed as one of the Big Four technology companies alongside Apple, Microsoft, and Google. The company is a billion-dollar global giant, with revenues reported in their fourth quarter of 2019 as $87.4 billion, with net income of $3.3 billion and earnings per share as $6.47.[2]

*USA Today* reports Amazon as being number three on Wall Street's twenty-five most valuable global corporate brands, with a brand value of $100.76 billion.

Needless to say, Amazon has made a place in history and hopes to keep delivering smiles for years to come.

---

[2] "Amazon reports $87.4 billion in Q4 2019 revenue: AWS up 34%, subscriptions up 32%, and 'other' up 41%," Venturebeat, accessed October 23, 2020, https://venturebeat.com/2020/01/30/amazon-earnings-q4-2019/.

# BECOMING AN AMAZON FLEX DRIVER

My mother, having worked in the restaurant industry for a majority of her life, is used to hearing all the latest news and trends that find their ways onto the American stage at any given time. After talking with a coworker, my mother was amazed to discover what the potential earnings were for Amazon Flex drivers. She decided to share this information with me, hoping it could be a way of providing additional income to our family of five. With my husband working full-time and me being a stay-at-home mom of our three boys, I had been praying and trying to find ways that I, too, could help provide for the family.

After hearing about the program from my mother, I decided to do my research. Amazon Flex was started in 2015 and now operates in about fifty US cities. It's a rideshare opportunity that allows everyday people to deliver packages and groceries through an app on their smartphones to other Amazon customers in surrounding cities. The program is similar to Uber and Lyft, as you conduct the "last-mile" delivery of the package from an Amazon regional warehouse directly to the customer.[3]

After better understanding the program, I began watching YouTube videos of other Flex drivers' pick-up and deliver routes. After viewing several deliveries, I began feeling confident that this was something I could definitely do. What was even more appealing about the job was that I was able to bring both my husband and our children along as I delivered packages! After explaining to my husband how everything worked, and that I felt this could really help provide for us (although he still wasn't 100 percent

[3] "How To Make Money On The Side With Amazon Flex," Listen Money Matters, accessed October 23, 2020, https://www.listenmoneymatters.com/amazon-flex/.

sure this was the path we should take), I decided to sign up. After months of waiting for my background check to go through and for all my paperwork to process, I finally was able to begin picking up shifts. Although it was God's plan to bring this program into my life, it wouldn't be until later that I would discover how much He planned to change my life with just a simple app on my phone!

# TIME TO DELIVER

Once I was able to log into the app, I was thrilled to discover one of the warehouses I could pick up packages from was three minutes from our house. When you pick up a shift from Amazon, they come in blocks of time. It ranges anywhere from two hours to four and a half hours. That is the allotted time Amazon gives you to complete your deliveries. Some routes can take less time than what you're given, and others longer. After looking at what shifts were available to me, I picked up my first four-and-a-half-hour block.

My husband and I agreed we both should go for my

first experience doing this, just in case I needed any help on the road. Plus with him driving, it would allow me to focus more on learning the process of doing the deliveries. When we arrived at the warehouse, we learned that the route you're given is randomly chosen. In other words, once you've parked, an Amazon warehouse employee brings over a cart full of packages to any surrounding city for you to deliver. You don't get to choose. In fact, I had assumed that I would only be delivering to the city I lived in. That was incorrect! I guess I missed that detail in the videos I watched. Therefore, I was stunned to discover they could send you to cities that were forty-five minutes or more away from your pick-up location. Moreover, if you were unable to deliver a package for whatever reason, you had to return it to the warehouse you picked up from after you made all your other deliveries. Again, these were details I had apparently missed.

The route we were given was to Edmonds, Washington. We both knew that city, and it wasn't too far, so that was encouraging. I learned the process pretty quickly, and we finished doing all the deliveries in about three and a half hours. We were excited that we finished early. *Perfect,* I thought. *This is working out.* I continued picking up several more shifts in the weeks ahead and began enjoying the work and the additional income. Then one day my husband and I got a route to a city we hadn't gone before, and things did *not* go as usual.

CHAPTER

FOUR

# WHAT IS HAPPENING?

My baby sister had agreed to watch the boys for us that afternoon so my husband and I could go out on a route that day. We arrived at our pick-up time and were given the city of Snohomish, Washington, for our deliveries. Snohomish is a large rural area that was close to where we lived, so we figured we would finish early. And that's exactly what we told my sister over the phone as we headed out.

Our initial deliveries went well. But as we began moving deeper into the area, the app began losing its signal, and the navigation system stopped working. Everyone who's close to me knows that when I do a job,

I want to do it perfectly and as efficiently as possible; I aim to be the best, not out of a competitive heart, but just because of the simple fact that it's important to me to perform well. Numerous times in my life I can remember so many job reviews where I was told that although I did work that was satisfactory, I needed to learn to slow down. So when I discovered Amazon Flex, I was so excited to find something where moving quickly was a good thing! So when the app stopped working and it was taking much longer than normal, I slowly began to stress and become frantic. I began worrying that I wasn't getting it done fast enough. Therefore, I wasn't performing to my standards of perfection.

We had to close out the application several times and reboot the system, hoping to regain the signal. We pulled over numerous times, as it would work for a few minutes and then go out again. We had to call Amazon Support for additional help with scanning the packages due to the lost signal, and it became more than I could handle. I was reduced to tears on several occasions during the route. Especially when I discovered my sister had somewhere to be, and we were taking much longer than what we had told her. As I cried, I kept asking my husband, "Why is

God allowing this? Why isn't He making the signal work? Doesn't He know we need to be back at a certain time?" Needless to say that route had become a disaster, and I couldn't wait for it to be over. Because I was so upset at how things went, I hadn't noticed that God still allowed us to finish the route in the allotted time frame of my block. Of course, I couldn't see that because we didn't finish when I wanted to finish.

After that day, anytime I went to the warehouse and was given the city of Snohomish, I became fearful and would even cry, trying to get out of it. I did not want to relive that experience. It became so bad that I began praying, "God, please don't let me get Snohomish," every time I drove to the warehouse. I'd tell God, "I want to work. I just don't want that city!"

Thank the Lord I didn't get Snohomish every time I went, and over time, I became faster and more proficient with my deliveries. Although I was growing in some areas, I still had the fear of being sent to Snohomish or any other destination where my phone wouldn't be able to pick up a clear signal. I was scared that I'd be stranded and unable to finish as quickly as I desired.

Looking back, I realized that God planned to use this

particular warehouse to help me become more efficient with the process of making deliveries before He began the process of helping deliver me from this fear. He wanted to provide me with training and experience because He knew something even harder was coming.

# THE BIG OPENING

After working at this specific warehouse for about five months, learning the trade and developing my skills, I was excited to hear that a new Amazon warehouse was opening about fifteen minutes from where we lived. When shifts began appearing for this new warehouse, I was thrilled to see that they offered times that were much different than the current warehouse I was working at. Plus, they offered more money. I soon found out this warehouse stayed open twenty-four hours; my current warehouse did not. In fact, they had shifts that began as early as 4:00 a.m. These early morning shifts really appealed to me because it allowed me to work while everyone was sleeping. Therefore, I would get more time with the family during the day. Seeing this as a huge opportunity, I jumped right in and picked up my first shift.

I was excited to see that many of the cities I was being sent to from this new warehouse were fairly close to my city. I also began a new process of learning how to deliver packages in the dark. I really enjoyed my work at this time, and the lack of traffic at 4:00 a.m. was remarkable. However, after about a month of doing deliveries, a new section of a certain city came on to the scene that would completely send me in a downward spiral.

# I'M BEING SENT WHERE?

I picked up another route as usual one morning and was off on my own while my husband and boys were still asleep. When I got the warehouse and was given my cart of packages, I noticed the city was Seattle. I had been sent to certain parts of Seattle by the previous warehouse I worked at, so I wasn't too concerned as I loaded each package into my car. There were about twenty-five packages or so for me to deliver. As I began driving, I saw the exit the GPS was telling me to take off our main freeway (I-5) was to downtown Seattle. I had never been to this part of the city, and I was amazed to see that this warehouse received routes to there. I knew of other Amazon warehouses that were much closer to this area, so I figured a route like this would be given to drivers from those locations.

When I arrived, I slowly began noticing that all my packages were to customers who lived in apartments. I obviously wasn't paying close enough attention to those details when I left the warehouse that morning. I then discovered that apartments in downtown Seattle were much different from the typical apartments I was used to delivering to. When you become an Amazon Flex driver, you learn very quickly that delivering to apartments is much different than delivering to a private residence. Each apartment complex has its own set of rules as to how packages can be delivered. They can range from having to drop deliveries to the leasing office, directly to the customer, or some other location on the property.

As I began making my deliveries, I soon realized all the apartments were in buildings that were locked to outside residents, and the parking with one-way streets everywhere was surreal. I noticed that each package would take me five minutes or more. Once I found parking outside the building, I had to review the information provided to me for getting inside. Once inside, I would either have to find the location where I had to drop the package on the main floor or take it directly to the customer's door. Most buildings contained numerous floors, which required an elevator ride or climbing multiple levels of stairs. Then I would find myself running around trying to find the specific apartment listed on the package. In some cases I had no information as to how to gain access to the building, which resulted in me having to contact the customer from the call box outside or by phone.

All these new procedures took what felt like hours to learn and understand. It got to the point that I again began stressing and becoming frantic. With previous routes, I only felt successful when I looked at the clock and saw that I had delivered a good amount of my packages since the time I left the warehouse. In this particular situation, I continued looking at the time and feeling like I had only delivered one package, and it had already been ninety minutes. By the time I got down to my last package, it had been about four and a half hours, and I was literally laughing in disbelief. I could not believe how this route had gone and how long it had taken me. Thank goodness my husband didn't have to be at work until later that morning and was able to get our boys on the bus to school. Needless to say, I never wanted to go to downtown Seattle again. Never!

As time went on, I of course again began asking God to please make sure He didn't send me back to Seattle every time I was given a cart of packages. However, I began to notice that regardless of my prayer request, downtown Seattle kept coming.

On another occasion, my husband and I decided to pick up a route together with our boys, and once more we were assigned to downtown Seattle. We were given twenty-four packages. I cried in the car as we drove down, dreading how long it would take us. I was also worried at the thought of how our boys would be stuck in the car for so long. Surprisingly, though, we worked together and were able to finish in two and a half hours. Once more I was so wrapped up in remembering how bad my initial route had gone that I hadn't noticed that I learned to navigate the city and even remembered certain details that helped save us time. Although our deliveries went pretty smooth that night, the fear of being sent back to downtown still lingered inside me, and it only got worse.

On another occasion, I picked up a route at 7:00 p.m. and was given about thirty packages to downtown. In a panic, I went back inside and explained to the warehouse personnel that I had delivered to this area before and with the number of packages I was assigned, I wouldn't be able to finish until late at night. On hearing this and seeing the terror written on my face, they allowed me to take fifteen packages instead. The route ended up taking me two and a half hours to complete. Much longer than I had hoped.

The fear finally became so bad that it began to cloud my judgment, and I actually began putting my job at risk. Without even knowing the exact number of packages I had in my cart one morning, I finally told myself, "This is too many," when I realized I was once more being sent to downtown Seattle. Overcome with anxiety, I took the cart of packages back into the warehouse and asked to speak to a manager. When the manager came over, I explained to him that I could not go to Seattle that morning because I had to be back at home to get my children ready for school. The manager told me that all they had were Seattle routes that morning, and if I couldn't go, I was going to need to talk to Amazon Support (the department in charge of Amazon Flex) and tell them what was going on. I called Support and explained the situation. They kindly told me this could only be a one-time occurrence, and it didn't look good on my record. At that moment I didn't seem to care that my perfect record could possibly be jeopardized by my actions. I was just so relieved that I wasn't going to downtown Seattle.

I ended up having to write an apology about my constant complaining to one of the warehouse personnel responsible for assigning carts to drivers during morning routes. I would complain that I was being given too many packages and that something must be wrong with the system. This would then result in me holding up the line and stopping her from completing her work. My fear had taken me down a path away from God and from clear thinking. What was happening to me?

To my surprise, God was sending me back to Seattle on purpose! He wanted me to learn and understand the process of how to deliver successfully to such a difficult area and that He would help me if I simply asked Him. He just needed me to trust Him and have the willingness to go. Which at those particular moments, I was not willing to go!

Following these incidents, I began having dreams where I could clearly hear the Lord's voice telling me, "You're not trusting Me!" I would wake up feeling awful, telling the Lord, "I know, I know." Why didn't God realize that it was just too hard and that I didn't want to go to Seattle? Why couldn't He just give me another city of my choice, where I wouldn't have to deal with parking and apartments? Why wouldn't it just go away?

I guess I just hadn't realized how bad it had become. God knew it was going to take drastic measures to fix it, and He had been formulating a plan behind all these previous mishaps I was trying to evade.

# HELP! HELP! HELP!

I got up one morning in a great mood and drove to the warehouse ready for another day. I noticed I hadn't gone to downtown for some time, so I was looking forward to another nearby city. The warehouse employee checking in drivers that morning knew me and noticed my happy glow as she commented, "You're in a good mood this morning!" I smiled and took my cart to my car and started unloading. As I scanned each package, I began to recognize the all too familiar streets of downtown Seattle. From my previous routes I remembered that it was better to sort the packages by street than by customer name because you often had multiple packages on the same street. A driver who was next to me loading packages in his car asked me where I was being sent. I looked at him and said, "Downtown Seattle." The look of both sadness and worry written on his face told me he was obviously being sent elsewhere.

I was so focused on organizing my packages that I forgot to count how many I had. When I finished scanning, I looked down at the total and saw that I had scanned forty packages! The driver next to me must have felt really bad for me because he offered to take my empty cart back into the warehouse. No one had ever done that for me before. There was no way I was getting out of this one. I had already used up all my excuses and free passes. God finally had me cornered to where the only thing I had left, was Him!

As I got into my car and began driving to Seattle. I started bawling and telling God how scared I was to go on this route. I just kept saying, "God, I'm scared! God, I'm scared!" I began trying to recount every situation in the Bible where God had done a miracle. I recited Psalm 34: "The righteous person has many troubles but the Lord delivers them from them all" (Psalm 34: 19 NIV). I did this all while thinking, *I only had twenty-five packages my first time, and it took over four hours. The other time only fifteen packages, and it took two and a half hours. How much time is forty packages going to take?* You could imagine my horror. I began shouting in the car, "God, show me what You can do! Show me what You can do!" At that moment I didn't care about my dignity. I was desperate!

With all these thoughts swirling in my head, I arrived at my first stop. I recognized the area and remembered that I previously had a hard time getting in this building because I was not given any information. However, this time I noticed directions were provided to me as to how to get in. I got it delivered!

My next delivery had information from the customer for accessing the building, but for some reason it wasn't working. I tried contacting the customer but was unable to reach them. I circled back and forth between the building's main doors and was unsuccessful. At that point I knew I was going back to the warehouse after my other deliveries because I was unable to deliver this package, which would take an additional thirty minutes. *Don't panic, Michelle, don't panic! God is going to help you. It's going to be okay. Melting down won't help!*

The next drop-off had multiple packages, and once

again I recognized the building and remembered not having any details of how to get in. To my surprise, after getting the packages unloaded, someone was there to meet me who was coming out of the building at the same time I was arriving. They let me in as they recognized I was with Amazon and had deliveries for other residents. Praise God, I got them delivered.

As I looked down at my next stop, I remembered seeing a package in the back that was to a nearby street, and I wondered why I was being sent elsewhere instead of to that location. I pulled over and got the package out of the back. I soon discovered I had missed scanning that package into my route, something that hardly ever happened; therefore, I had forty-one to deliver, compared to the forty I had originally thought. I got the package scanned in and headed to that stop. On arriving I noticed I was being directed to a side door, where I could see the janitor of the building through the window. I knocked, made eye contact with him, and showed him the package in my hand. He met me at the door and directed me to where I needed to go to make the delivery. Thank goodness, another one completed!

As I headed back to my car, I noticed this package

was located right across the street from the package I was unable to deliver earlier. Since I was right there, I decided to give it another try. I grabbed the package and ran across the street. When I came to one of the doors, I was amazed to see someone standing in the lobby! I knocked on the door, and the resident looked over and began heading my way. She kindly opened the door, and recognizing who I was, directed me to the package room. I told God, "Thank you so much," as I dropped it off in the designated room. Yes, another one delivered!

I jumped back into my car and headed off to my next stop. This next building had two packages. With both in hand, I headed to the front door and began reading the notes provided to me. With the first package I looked at, I was told to contact the customer on arrival to gain access to the building. I tried multiple times and was unsuccessful. *God, help! God, help!* I then reviewed the other customer's information and was told the same thing. However, when I contacted this customer he answered and let me in the building. I delivered both packages! Thank the Lord!

I continued on. The next building again had multiple deliveries. With these packages in hand, I headed to the front doors. I tried contacting the customer and was unsuccessful. I circled the building, praying and refusing to give up. Once again, someone who was leaving for work met me at another set of doors just in time. They helped me get in the building and directed me to where I needed to leave the packages. Yes! Two more deliveries done!

The rest of the morning went the same way. Stop after stop. People were either coming out of the building at the same time I arrived, or I was given the information I needed to make the delivery. I made sure I didn't look at the clock while delivering that morning because I knew if I continued watching the time, I would begin to worry. Instead I just continued praying. I had to be back at our house that morning by 8:15 because my husband had to leave for work and was unable to get our boys off to school. My mom, who was usually available to help, had to be at a meeting that morning. Thus, I had to be home in time. What were the odds that I would get forty-one packages on the same morning I had a time restraint and had somewhere to be? God knew what He was doing!

I finally got down to my last package, and I saw it was to another apartment. There weren't any directions provided in the notes or information to get me into the building if it were locked. I had no idea what to expect.

When I arrived I saw it was a normal apartment complex, where residents access their apartments from the outside, not from within a locked building. I dropped it off without a problem. I had delivered all the packages! I didn't have to go back to the warehouse. I got back into my car and looked at the time. It was 7:45; I had finished my route in just under three hours.

As I was just coming to realization of what had happened, my phone rang. I picked up when I saw it was my husband and was crying tears of joy as I told him, "God did it! God did it! I can't believe it. He really did it!" God literally had parted the Red Sea for me! Thank You, Jesus! I rode in shock all the way home. I arrived around 8:15, just in time to get our kids up, dressed, fed, and out the door.

If I hadn't "missed" that package when scanning earlier, I would have never gone back to that other stop and would have had to go back to the warehouse. I think God did that on purpose as He knew someone would be there when I arrived the second time. If you were to ask any other Flex drivers, they would tell you that completing that number of package deliveries to downtown Seattle in under three hours without having to return any packages to the warehouse is literally a miracle! Especially during that time of day. It wasn't like people were home all day and readily available to receive their packages. In other words, God made what felt like the impossible, possible! I just couldn't believe it. That route changed my life.

CHAPTER
EIGHT

# ALL THINGS BECOME NEW

I never imagined how much that morning would change who I was and my relationship with God. The process was terrifying, but the results have been amazing. Since then, I've noticed a huge change in my thinking and countenance.

> Old Me: "What if I get sent to Seattle or Snohomish again? What if I get all apartments, or the signal doesn't work? What if it takes me four or five hours to complete the route? What if I have to go back to the warehouse? How am I going to get out of this?"

New Me: "Where I'm sent is where I'm sent. God, as long as You are there, I know it's going to be okay. This is the route You've chosen for me, so I know You have a plan. If the signal goes out, You can bring it back! If I have all apartments, you can send people to help me. If I have to go back to the warehouse, I know You'll provide me with plenty of extra time to do so.

In fact, now when I notice I'm being sent to downtown, I stay calm, remembering what He did that past morning. As I scan each package, I ask God, "Are You ready? Let's go!" I tell Him He's the best partner I could ever have, and I ask Him to send people ahead of me, just like He did before.

Since that route, I've seen it time and time again. I would arrive at an apartment complex with no idea where the front door was and have no notes or instructions on arriving. I would get out, and I would see someone in the parking lot going to a car. The person would see me and ask if I needed help. When I told the person what apartment unit I was trying to locate, the person would say, "Oh, wow, that's for me." I of course smile, and happily hand the individual the package. I then would get into my car with this huge smile on my face, knowing that God had moved ahead of me. I still ask Him how He does that. I remember the verse in Isaiah 52:12 (NIV) that states, "For the Lord will go before you, the God of Israel will be your rearguard." God is the only one who could ensure that the person whose package I had to deliver would be standing in the parking lot at the moment I arrived!

When you see this happen over and over, you become so aware of God's presence and His ability to control things that it gets to the point where it overwhelms you. It's unbelievable what He can do! Now when I hear other Flex drivers say, "I hope I don't get Seattle," I just laugh because I no longer have to fear that city. I know God comes with me and will help. He was there all along. I just didn't realize it because I was so busy panicking and trying to run away. Actually, I've come to like going to Seattle when God sends me because I get to see all the miracles He does. I'm so thankful God gave me the grace and courage not to give up. He wants the same for you!

# DON'T MISS OUT

It's one thing to read about how God parted the Red Sea for the Israelites, but it's a totally different experience when God parts the waters for you!

I think so many times God tries to do this for us as Christians, but we don't allow Him. In fact, we refuse! We mainly run away from these situations out of sheer fear and frustration. Derek Prince, my favorite Bible teacher would say, "If the same situation continues to appear in your life, you need to ask God, What do I need to learn?" I think so many times we think it's the enemy—Satan—trying to harm us or create problems in our lives. In reality, it's God trying to draw out areas in our characters that need to be dealt with. In this instance, it was my fear of not being able to perform perfectly, my reliance on my own abilities, my reliance on other people to bail me out, and my inability to trust God during my deliveries. Once I allowed God to take over and help, everything changed. The key was I had to be willing to go and willing to let Him do it. The routes I picked up from Amazon were an area in my life where God was able to control the outcome fully, from start to finish. He chooses the location each time, and He is the only one able to send people to help me when I need it. There is nothing more I can do except drive the car and go. He does the rest! As Paul states in 2 Corinthians 1:9 (NIV), "But as a result, we stopped relying on ourselves and learned to rely only on God, who raises the dead." When you realize how amazing He is at controlling one aspect of your life, you'll want to give Him a whole lot more!

I know these situations can be awful and terrifying. But don't give up and walk away. Maybe you're having the same recurring situation at your workplace, within your business, or in another area in your life. Can you think of any situations when you become fearful and anxious every time they occur? Do they make you stressed and overwhelmed?

Take some time to stop and ask God, "Is there anything You're trying to teach me in this?" I needed to go into these situations with the mindset that God was in control, and He can do all things. I had to believe this was really true in my heart and mind in order to get myself into the car that morning to deliver those forty-one packages. Otherwise, it was over. I was sunk. I lived out Romans 12:2 (NIV): "Do not conform to the pattern of this world, but be transformed by the renewing of your mind. Then you will be able to test and approve what God's will is—his good, pleasing and perfect will." When God renews one's mind, He typically takes you through a process of change. He doesn't just say to you, "Renew your mind." He actually has to change your mind through some circumstance or process within your life that can produce this transformation.

As you can see, God decided to use delivering for Amazon as a source for my needed change. Again, I just had to be a willing participant. That forty-one package route that morning was the giant step into my new way of thinking. But it took my willingness to go and step out in faith. Again, it's not easy at all, but it's worth it! I discovered in these moments that God's not as concerned with us being afraid as He is with how we act when we become fearful. Are we taking the time to stop and pray? Are we asking for His help? Are we going to everyone around us instead of God?

I could have just quit Amazon and walked away. I could have said, "This job is too hard. I should find something else that's easier. This isn't fair!" However, I would have missed what God was trying to do in my life. I would have lost the miracle and all the benefits that came with it.

Through all this, I've come to see once again that God is hilarious! He really does have a sense of humor. I still laugh when I think how much He changed my life with Amazon package delivery. I would have never imagined this would ever be an avenue He would use. I was so wrong! It was such an eye-opener when I realized that it was God's will for me to deliver for Amazon. It was His plan all along, from the very beginning. I didn't have to become ordained or do something extraordinary for my church. I just needed to find the path He wanted me to travel on—or in this case, deliver to. If God can use Amazon to change my life, just think what He can use to change your life.

I did not have the best attitude during this process of renewing my mind by any means. I have the heart of a five-year-old, so I complained to God constantly and had tantrums on the regular. However, I stuck with it, and He appreciated the honesty. God wants you to be honest with Him. Tell Him you're scared and that it's too much. He wants to know how you feel and to hear your heart. He knows these things aren't easy. How can it be easy when you feel like you're being put through a blender? Despite the pain, keep at it! Allow Him to walk with you through this process of change. Trust me, He'll deliver. Literally! You won't be disappointed.

In case you're wondering, I'm still delivering for Amazon. God continues to help me deliver to my fellow neighbors, even during COVID-19. Also, be sure to thank your Amazon delivery drivers every time you see them. The job is a lot harder than one may think. So hard in fact, that I have to call on the King of kings and the Lord of lords for help when making deliveries. Especially to you Seattleites! Hey, who knows? Maybe God will send me to your house next. If He does, please make sure I have all the information I need to get it to you!

Printed in the United States
By Bookmasters